What Leaders are saying about this book...

Through the art of storytelling, "The Tale of Two Team Members" shares timeless wisdom on what most believe to be the single largest challenge in building a sustainable business....leading team members. The sequential lessons vignette approach to the story not only makes it easy to follow, but more importantly, makes it easy for the reader to grasp the learnings in a logical flow. Regardless of where you are in your career, the lessons found within this book will make you better.

Rand Harbert
Chief Agency, Sales and Marketing Officer
State Farm Insurance Companies

*** *** *** ***

I read this book over the week-end and saw once more why you are so successful. Like other people that are successful, the book is a reminder that if you go back to the basics and you focus on execution you will be successful.

Denis Dubois
SVP & COO
Desjardins General Insurance Group subsidiaries.

A creative resource for your leadership tool kit to develop and empower great team members. Because your success depends on your expertise with positive accountability and aligning employees with your performance expectations – you'll want to learn this important tale.

David Hill
VP Agency
State Farm Canada Inc.

*** *** *** ***

The book is very well written. While it may seem to some readers, too simple, it is the simplicity of the topic that is key. Hiring, training, and maintaining employees that "Get It" is the most important objective of successful businesses. If an employee does not "Get It", it is best for everyone to move on. Excellent Employee Engagement leads to Great Client Experience which results in Increased Profitability.

George McCarter
President and Chief Marketing Officer
Jones Brown Inc.

*** *** *** ***

A Tale of Two Team Members and the Insurance Agent Who Wanted to Lead Them" by Dr. Chris Bart and insurance expert Wayne Nichols, provides a successful strategy to develop the necessary leadership skills to run any insurance agency. By answering four basic questions, this book assures that whoever is in charge of the team, will find the right tools to meet long term goals through positive leadership practices. This book is a unique guide, not only because of the answers it provides, but due to the way it is told. The fact that it is written as a story makes it easy to understand and to follow the authors' thinking process. It contains lots of great leadership tips for all sorts of environments. Definitely glad I read this one and I would HIGHLY recommend this book to all current and future leaders of insurance agencies. It should become a must-read for all of them, and the four questions process should be mandatory in every business school.

Sam Malatesta, C.Dir.
Founder & CEO, ClaimsCorp International
Chairman, Centre for Innovation & Leadership

*** *** *** ***

Any financial practice could benefit from the wisdom contained in this remarkable little book. I just wish 'A Tale of Two Team Members' had been around when I started my agency! It would have made my job as the leader of a small practice so much easier, and more profitable. No leader of an insurance agency should be without this book!

Paul J Vaneyk
Paul J. Vaneyk Financial Services
Peterborough, Ontario

A
Tale
of
Two
Team
Members

*& the Insurance Agent who wanted
to lead them.*

by

Dr. Chris Bart, FCPA
&
Wayne Nichols
Insurance & Financial Services Agent

*"Simple truths for getting almost
anyone to do what needs to be done"*

Dr. Chris Bart, FCPA

Phone: 905-515-6399

email: chrisbart@corporatemissionsinc.com

ISBN 978-0-9938801-2-4

For Robert, it was the best of times and it was the worst of times.

It was the best of times because he had been provided with an amazing opportunity. As a recent graduate of the insurance company's Agency Training Program, Robert was becoming an independent agent representing the insurance company. He had been assigned an existing Agency from which the agent had left suddenly, and he was excited to establish himself in the industry. Robert knew that it would not always be easy sailing, because leadership came with responsibility. Nevertheless, he was ready to prove that, given this opportunity, he could become one of the strongest agents within the company.

But it was also the worst of times because Robert worried that he was not going to do well, that he was going to FAIL!

And why?

Because Michael and Susan, two of his Agency's Client Care team members who had worked for the previous agent and had remained on, were for some reason *not doing what needed to be done.*

As front-line workers, Michael's and Susan's job was to answer the Agency's main telephone line and direct calls to other Agency members, but most importantly, to assist existing and potential clients with their insurance and financial services needs. According to Robert, this should have been a relatively straight-forward job to perform. "After all," he thought many times to himself, *"this isn't rocket science!"* And yet, based on the information that he had just received from a recent Client Telephone Quality Report, both Michael and Susan were not meeting the "expectations" of the Agency's clients.

Those expectations were embodied in the ***company's new mission statement***. It was posted on every wall and on the back of every business card. The company even had T-shirts made with the mission statement printed on it and had given one to each team member in every agent's office.

The new mission statement had been announced with a flourish of fanfare and inspiring speeches from the head office leadership. Everyone was told to ***embrace*** the mission, to ***live*** the mission statement ***and to make it their own***. It read:

Our Mission

is to provide insurance
products of the highest level
of quality and service that
will truly delight and amaze
each and every client we are
privileged to serve.

We are committed
to providing our team
members with opportunities
for learning and personal
growth.

Above all, team members
will be provided the same
respect, appreciation and
caring attitude that they are
expected to give each client.

We will recognize
achievement and be socially
responsible members
of the community.

After the mission was introduced, everyone in each agent's office was asked to sign a huge poster on which the mission was printed, thereby signifying each person's acceptance and support of it. Everyone in Robert's new Agency, including Michael and Susan, had signed it.

Robert had recently received a Client Telephone Quality Report which stated that clients were "DISSATISFIED" with their experience when telephoning his agency. They said their experience was not one of "delight" or "amazement".

"*Why won't they do what the company needs them to do?*" Robert asked himself. "They were present for the launch of the new mission. They even signed the mission statement declaration. Why are they holding back and resisting?"

Robert was unsure what to do. Since this was the first time that he had ever managed others, he did not want to make any mistakes. He knew that being a good team leader held the key to his success as an agent. And so he knew that if he got off on the wrong foot with these two team members, his plans for running a successful Agency could be jeopardized … And Robert liked the career path that he was on.

Because he was a clever young man, Robert decided to consult Philip - a wise old man who had been an agent with the company for many, many years. Robert had met Philip when he attended several of Philip's lectures at Agency School.

Everyone respected Philip because Philip always got the job done. His authority flowed not just from his success as a leading agent, but from the respect others had for him. Philip had a reputation as a team leader who brought out the best in people. And, according to Robert's informal sources, Philip was already seen as the person who was excelling at driving home the new mission in his Agency.

"I should talk with Philip", thought Robert. So he called the wise old man to arrange a convenient time to chat.

Philip told Robert to come by immediately.

The First Question

When Robert arrived at Philip's office, he was greeted warmly by the wise old man. Philip liked Robert. He saw Robert as a clever young man with great potential to be an excellent agent. It made Philip happy to think that he might play a role in helping to make that happen.

"So," asked Philip, "what's the problem that you need to see me about? I would have thought that after Agency School you didn't need any more advice from an old man like me. You appeared to have everything down pat. But, I'm always glad to see you and happy to help in any way that I can."

"Thanks, Philip," replied Robert. "But back at Agency School, you taught me that it is never wrong to seek out anyone's opinion when you have a problem that you're not sure how to solve. As a matter of fact, you impressed upon me the view that a person should get as many opinions from as many experienced agents like yourself when faced with a challenge."

Philip laughed, "Okay," he said, "you've learned your lessons from me very well. But, enough of the flattery young man. What can I do for you?"

Robert explained his managerial dilemma, "I have two Client Care team members whose main responsibilities center around their telephone conversations with the Agency's clients. This morning I was reviewing a Client Telephone Quality Report and I was disappointed to learn that these team members are not living up to the expectations articulated in company's mission statement. The report says that our clients are very dissatisfied with the service they have been receiving from Michael and Susan."

"I see," said Philip. Then, after a few seconds of silence he asked, "But, *do they know what to do?*"

"Do they know what to do?" a perplexed Robert repeated. "Well, they should!" he exclaimed. "Both Michael and Susan were present when the new mission was unveiled. They both heard the speeches. They both signed the poster. I've even seen Michael wearing the new T-shirt with the mission statement printed on it. There is also a plaque containing the company's mission statement right behind each of their desks that they would see every day when they come to work. So, I would say that they both know what to do."

Philip, who was watching Robert's animated response closely, replied quietly, "Yes, Robert, I hear what you are saying, but let me ask you again: Do Michael and Susan really *know what to do?*"

"I'm not quite sure I understand what you mean." Robert asked haltingly.

"Well then, let me try to be more clear," replied Philip. "Do Michael and Susan know the new mission statement?"

"Know the new mission statement? Of course they know it", replied Robert, somewhat peeved with Philip's persistent question. "How could they not know it given all that we have done to communicate it to them?"

"You're right", Philip replied. "They should know it. But, before we continue, why don't you go and check this out for yourself, just to be sure. Besides, I really have to get back to my own work right now since my Sales Leader needs to see me in around forty-five minutes. Come back and see me tomorrow when you've had a chance to find out the answer to my question. Okay?"

"Alright," said Robert. And with that, the two men shook hands. Robert then returned to his Agency where it was late in the day, almost quitting time. Robert decided to act while the conversation with the wise old man was still fresh in his head.

He called his two team members into his office. "Michael, Susan … " he began, "I know this might seem like a dumb question, but, uh … you both know about the new mission statement … right?"

"Oh, sure we do!" chimed Susan. "We all remember the big party that we had way back when to introduce it. It was a lot of fun."

"The bosses from head office gave some pretty good speeches." echoed Michael. "Some of the better ones that they've ever made, I might add. My wife also really liked the T-shirt. She said it is made of a high-quality cotton."

Robert braced himself as he prepared for his next words. "I'm glad you remember that a new mission statement was introduced a while back. But, do you remember what the mission statement said exactly? Do either of you remember any of the words in it?" He held his breath.

"Well ... uh ... not really," said Michael.

"Didn't it pretty well say much of the same old stuff ... something about the client?" asked Susan. "Not much new in my opinion!"

"Philip was right," thought Robert as he bowed his head in despair. "They don't know the mission statement. They don't *know what to do.*" At that, he said, "Thanks guys. Let's call it a day."

On the car ride home that night, Robert reflected on his conversation with Philip and what had happened with Michael and Susan.

The next day, Robert phoned his new mentor Philip and arranged a time to resume their discussion. As Robert entered Philip's office, the wise old man boomed, "So, my clever young man, how did it go with Michael and Susan?"

"Just as you suspected," a dejected Robert answered, "they don't **know what to do** because they don't know the mission statement. But that surprises me after everything that the company has done to make sure that we all know about the new mission statement."

"Does it really?" replied Philip. "Did you really think that once all the hoopla died down about the new mission statement that it would have any impact or relevance? Oh sure, the company did a fine job acquainting everyone with the mission statement and informing us that there was a new one. They did all the usual stuff. And the company should be commended for this because some organizations expect their team members to be mind readers when it comes to knowing their important messages ..."

"But, what they did could hardly be called *effective communication*. In fact, it's been my experience that just because someone has an important message, like a mission statement, to send out to the rest of the organization, and it has been *sent*, it doesn't always necessarily follow that the message will automatically be heard or *received*, let alone *remembered* by the sender's intended audience. And, when you think about it, *if people have not heard a message, especially an important one such as the company's mission statement, they can't even begin to live it and they won't know what to do.* Now for a message to be received and remembered, you have to take a few extra steps."

"Like what?" asked Robert.

"Like *relentlessly repeating* the mission statement!" exclaimed Philip. "You have to *recite it and repeat it over and over again* so that no one forgets it. And it needs to be referred to all the time. It's just not enough to have the mission statement printed on plaques, business cards, team member manuals, screen savers and T-shirts. You found that out for yourself with Michael and Susan. A mission statement or any other important message needs to be imprinted onto your brain if it's going to have any impact. This will make the message real and then it will be remembered."

"Interesting," Robert interjected. "And how exactly do you go about doing that?"

"Well," the wise old man replied, "we do a lot of things."

"Such as ...?"

"To begin with," said Philip, "I told each of my Agency team members - about 10 people - that I expected them to memorize the new mission statement. I also told them that I would approach each of them on a random basis and ask them to recite it on the spot. If they could recite it, I would buy them a coffee. If they couldn't, then I would try to recite the mission statement myself. If I could, then they would need to buy me a coffee. If I couldn't, I would still need to buy them the coffee. Sometimes, I made the bet for lunch or some other reward ... such as washing their car on my lunch break."

"But you also mentioned that you refer to it a lot. How do you do that?" asked Robert.

"That's a bit harder ... because you always have to be vigilant for opportunities to do so ... take birthday celebrations, for instance. I used to have little informal parties for my team members simply because we all liked doing it. Today, though, I always make a point of remarking to my team that the reason why we have these parties is because it's just another one of the small ways in which I try to show the '*appreciation and caring attitude*' embodied in our mission statement. By taking this approach, we can connect our specific actions to the mission statement and people can see that the words are not fake ... that the words are real ..."

"But, now, let me ask you this," Philip continued,

"and please forgive me for being cruel when I say this ... but, Robert, do you know the company's mission statement? ... Can you tell me what it says?"

"What do you mean?" stammered the clever young man.

"I mean," Philip replied, "can you recite the mission statement for me?"

"You want me to recite the mission statement for you ...? here ...? Right now ...?"

"Yes." replied Philip with a hint of sarcasm in his voice. "Recite the company's mission statement for me ... if you can."

Robert began slowly, "The mission statement of our company is ... is ... is to ... to provide ... high quality service ... to all of our clients ... all the time. Or something very close to that ... right?"

"Not really." said Philip who then recited the mission statement perfectly for Robert.

"Robert," he continued. "I'm really quite disappointed in your answer because the first thing that good leaders learn is *never to ask a subordinate or a team member to do anything that they are not prepared to do themselves.* **A good leader leads by example.** How can you expect Michael and Susan to take the mission statement seriously when you aren't even doing so yourself?"

"You're right", said Robert as he made a mental note to himself to learn the mission statement by heart that afternoon.

"But, is there anything else that I can do to help my team members remember the mission?" inquired Robert.

"Oh sure." Philip replied. "For instance, we usually begin our weekly staff meeting with everyone reciting the mission statement en masse. We have even begun having occasional 'mission statement quizzes' in which we give everyone a copy of the mission statement with key words deleted and then ask each person to individually fill in the blanks. We then post the ranked results on the department bulletin board for everyone to see."

Philip then reached into his desk drawer and pulled out a sheet of paper.

He handed it to Robert.

On the page was the company's mission statement written as follows:

The Mission Statement Quiz

Our mission
is to provide -------- of
the ------- level of
------- and -------
that will ----- ------- and -----
---- and every --------
we are ---------- to -----.
We are ---------
to providing our --------- with
opportunities for -------- and ---
- ---
Above all, team
members will be --------
with the same -------, ----------
and --------- attitude
that they are --------
to give each --------.
We will recognize ----------- and
be -------- ----------- members of the

"And this works?" asked Robert.

"Let's go see for yourself," the wise old man answered and at that, he got up, motioned for Robert to follow him and walked out of his office. The first desk they stopped at was Philip's secretary, Betty.

"Betty," said Philip, "this is Robert and I've been telling him all about our efforts to learn the company's new mission statement. Can you recite it for him?" Betty smiled and with absolutely no effort, the words of the company mission statement rolled off her lips. Philip then asked Robert to randomly approach three other team members from the work area and to ask them to recite the mission statement. Each sailed through the request. Robert was impressed and vowed to himself that, someday soon, Michael and Susan would be able to do the same. "They, too, will **know what to do**," he thought.

Robert then thanked the wise old man for his time and professed his eagerness in getting back to his own Agency so that he could begin putting into practice some of the ideas that he had learned. Philip told him to come back anytime if the clever young man had any other concerns.

Over the next several weeks, Robert worked diligently at making sure that both Michael and Susan knew the mission statement. He told them that he expected them to memorize it.

Michael, however, complained that he thought the mission statement was too hard to memorize because it was "much too long!" Robert was prepared for this, though, and when he recited the mission statement for both team members, Michael's jaw dropped.

"You must have a good memory," exclaimed Michael. "I could never do that!"

"Actually, Michael, I have a lousy memory," Robert replied, "but, I thought about some of the stuff that I've memorized in the past. The pledge of allegiance, for instance. Some prayers. And even the words to a favorite song. I suddenly realized that the only way that I learned them by heart was by first, committing to learn them and second, by *relentlessly repeating the words, over and over again* until I had it right. That's all there is to memorizing anything. I did it and so can you".

Robert then promised that he would help both team members memorize the mission statement. In fact, he challenged them to a free coffee the next day if they both could recite it correctly.

Robert was only half disappointed. Michael came in with the mission statement well memorized. Susan, on the other hand, said that she had forgotten all about it. She promised, though, to have it memorized by lunch but, then, stumbled through it. Robert told Susan that he expected her to do better. Susan promised that she would "know it cold" and "have it nailed" the next day - which, she did.

Thereafter, Robert made it a regular practice to have "mission statement drills" and he even "borrowed" the wise old man's mission statement quiz and used it, as a bet, to see who would have to go and fetch lunch for the three of them.

Time passed and Robert, being a clever young man, grew increasingly confident of both team members' ability to know the mission statement. "They now *know what to do.*" said Robert a bit smugly to himself. "The message has been sent. The message has been received. And the message has been remembered. Philip would be very proud of me."

Imagine Robert's surprise, then, when after several more weeks, the next Client Telephone Quality Report was issued and, based on the statistics, it indicated that there was virtually no change in the ratings for Robert's Agency. Clients were still reporting being "DISSATISFIED" with the quality and level of service being received when telephoning his Agency.

"This is not possible," cried Robert. "Michael and Susan both know the mission statement." To confirm this, he jumped up from behind his desk and walked over to the doorway where he spotted Susan. "Quick, Susan," he said, "what's the company's mission statement?"

"That's easy," Susan replied and she rhymed off the sentences flawlessly. Then Susan added, "How did I do, boss?"

"Great Susan. Just great." responded Robert, but without the usual enthusiasm in his voice.

"Then what's wrong?" asked Susan.

"I'm not sure." answered Robert as he quickly darted towards the door leading to the parking lot and his car.

A short while later, Robert found himself standing outside Philip's office. Philip's door was ajar and he was just hanging up his telephone.

Robert stuck his head inside the office and asked with just a tinge of anxiousness in his voice, "Got a moment, Philip?"

Philip could see that Robert was somewhat upset, so he said, "Sure Robert, but I've only got about five minutes. Is it urgent?"

"Sort of...." Robert said. "You remember our previous conversation about my two team members that I was concerned about ... Michael and Susan? Well, I've just reviewed my Agency's latest Client

Telephone Quality Report and the results indicate that clients are still not happy with their experience when telephoning into my Agency. So, I don't understand what's going on Philip, How can this be happening?"

"*Do they know what to do?*" the wise old man asked.

"Do they know what to do?" repeated Robert almost shouting. "Of course, they know what to do. I have done everything that we talked about the last time. I have told them that I needed them to memorize the mission statement. And they have done it. We recite it all of the time. Susan even just did it for me moments before I came to see you. So, they know the mission statement….The message has been sent. The message has been received. The message is remembered… But they still aren't doing what needs to be done."

"I see," said Philip. "But let me try something with you, Robert. I am going to say some words for you. Okay? Here they are: 'dog', 'cat', 'flower', 'tree'."

"Dog, cat, flower, tree?" repeated Robert quizzically.

"That's right," the wise old man responded. "Dog, cat, flower, tree. When I say those words, tell me what is happening inside your brain. If I am not mistaken, you actually see a picture of a cat or dog or flower or tree."

"You're right," said Robert.

Philip continued, "We think best when we think in pictures … when we can 'see' what is being said. Now, let me say some other words for you, Robert. 'Highest quality', 'highest service', 'truly delight and amaze'. Tell me what you 'see' when I say some of the key words from our company's new mission statement to you?"

"Nothing," responded Robert, "I see nothing. Just fog."

"And if YOU only see fog when I say those words, Robert, then just imagine what Michael and Susan see."

"Probably the same thing," Robert replied weakly.

"Absolutely," boomed Philip. "So when I asked you '*Do they know what to do?*' the real answer should have been 'No, they don't'. Yes, *the mission statement has been sent, received and remembered.* But it still has not been **understood** to the point where Michael and Susan can '*see*' what the words actually *mean*.

"As a matter of fact Robert, I also have to confess a bit of a bias when it comes to saying things a certain way. I actually prefer and value the phrase "*I see*" more than the phrase "I understand" because you can 'understand' the need for client satisfaction and yet, still not 'see' what it entails or what it involves ... And so, only when someone can 'see' what it is that they are supposed to do will they really be able to say that they **know what to do.**"

"I think I'm beginning to understand ... er, I mean, I SEE," Robert chuckled. "But how can I get them to 'see' the mission statement?"

"Now, Robert, that's part of what being a leader is all about," responded Philip with a hint of impatience growing in his voice. "**Leaders help others translate the words in the mission statement so that they have meaning for them.** So that others can say 'I see'."

"And do you have any advice on how I should go about doing this?" asked Robert.

"Sure Robert, there are many things that you could do. But, my time with you is running out ... So why don't you come back and see me tomorrow around 11:30 am?" And at that, Philip flew out the door leaving Robert to ponder everything that the wise old man had said.

Before driving back to his office, Robert jotted some notes on the pad of paper that he was carrying:

Robert's Notes...

In order for team members to **know what to do**, a leader must **communicate effectively** with them. A leader should make sure that:

- The message containing what team members are expected to do is **sent** (team members are not mind readers). This is one of the purposes of mission.

- The message is **received**. Just because a message is sent does not mean that it has been heard. Test for active listening.

- The message is **understood**. The message should be clear and have meaning so that team members can say '**I see**'. *Leaders help others to translate the words*.

- The message is **remembered**. Relentlessly repeating over and over again important messages helps to keep them current and alive. A message not remembered is the same as a message not sent.

- *Leaders lead by example.*
  Leadership comes with responsibility. If the message is not sent, received, understood or remembered, team members **WILL NOT KNOW WHAT TO DO!**

The next day, Robert returned to Philip's office to pick up where they had left off. "You were about to explain how I might help Michael and Susan better **understand** the mission statement, **to see what it means,** so that they will **know what to do.**" Robert began.

"That's right," replied the wise old man, "and there are many things that you might do. But, let me turn your question back on you. **How do you think you might** go about helping Michael and Susan translate the mission message so that it has meaning for them? ... so that they will **know what to do** when it comes to living the mission? What are some of the things that you could do to help them?" Philip then grabbed for a pad of paper on his desk and handed it to Robert.

"Here," he said, "**write down all of the things that you might possibly do to answer this question** ... and DON'T pre-judge your ideas. Just write them down as quickly as possible."

After about two minutes, Robert handed the page with his answers on it back to the wise old man. It read:

Robert's List

1. Tell Michael and Susan what I think the mission statement words mean and tell them what I specifically want them to do.

2. Do a client survey to find out what clients expect given the words in the mission statement and then inform Michael and Susan.

3. Ask Michael and Susan what they think the words of the mission statement mean.

4. Do all of the above.

"That's a great list," smiled Philip. "Now, which one should you do?"

"The one that I want to do is to simply tell Michael and Susan what to do." replied Robert.

"Why?" inquired the wise old man.

"Because, that's what a leader does, right? I have to let them know who is in charge so that they will know that I am the boss. Besides, it's also the quickest solution. "

"It may be quick," replied Philip, "but it can also be extremely costly ... the reason being that taking your approach presumes that you are right ... that you always have the correct answer ... which, of course, you may not ... and if you don't, you'll look like an idiot in the eyes of Michael and Susan ... Yet, don't get me wrong, Robert, you should still make sure that you have your own ideas about how the words translate as well."

"So, then, if I read you right," interjected Robert, "I should probably first try to do a client survey to find out what my clients want and how they would interpret the words in our mission statement. Only then will I really know the correct meaning of the words."

"You could, you should and you must do that. The client's perspective is vital. But there are several things that you need to bear in mind as you do the survey. The first is that the client may not know what he or she wants ... or may not be able to express it. The other problem that might emerge is that it may take some time organizing the survey or focus group, collecting the data and interpreting the results. And, it will, for sure, if you ask your Sales Leader to organize it for you. In the meantime, you can expect your clients to still be "DISSATISFIED" with their experience when telephoning into the company. So, my advice to you is to, at least, try to do it yourself while you wait for their report confirming - or denying - what you have found."

"I see," said Robert, "so, are you saying that the "correct answer" is number three?"

Philip laughed, "I'm not telling you anything, Robert. I'm just **helping** you and me arrive at a preferred alternative. Now, think about it. What are some of the advantages from asking Michael and Susan for their thoughts?"

"To begin with," said Robert, "I get to hear their ideas and see if they have any that might be better than mine."

"Absolutely!" roared Philip. "But there's another advantage which is probably just as important."

"And what's that?" inquired Robert.

"It's how Michael or Susan will feel if you adopt any of their suggestions or proposed solutions and then give them credit for it. How do you think that it would make them feel, Robert?"

"I would guess pretty good," replied Robert.

"Not just pretty good, Robert, but GREAT!" bellowed Philip, "and why? Because they want what everyone wants: *to feel good about themselves, to feel important, to feel that their opinion counts and that what they do here matters*. In other words, *everyone wants to feel respected, valued, and appreciated*. That's why we say what we do in our mission statement. Robert ... you know, the part that goes: 'Above all, team members will be provided the same respect, appreciation and caring attitude that they are expected to give each client.' We believe that everyone wants this and, from what I have read, all the research on team member satisfaction tends to support this."

"I see," said Robert.

"And so, Robert, one of the possible ways we might try to satisfy this need that all team members feel," Philip continued, "is *by asking them questions* ... by asking for their ideas and opinions ... and by acknowledging and thanking them for their contributions. When I do this, my people know that *I need them and that I depend on them for getting things done. They feel 'worth-full', not worthless."*

"But what if they give you a dumb answer? Or, one that you think is incorrect or stupid...? Then what do you do?"

"Now, let me turn the question back on you, Robert," replied Philip. "What do you think a wise leader should do in this situation?"

"Probably ask **WHY** they think the way that they do," answered Robert.

"Precisely," said Philip, "because once you hear their rationale, you might not think that it's such a dumb idea anymore. But if it does, in fact, turn out to be a 'less than perfect' response, then 'asking why' will begin to highlight the flaws in their logic or rationale. You can then phrase your 'objections' in the form of other probing questions that might help your team members *see*. Questions such as 'Have you thought about ...?' or 'What about ...?' or 'Did you consider ...?' That way if they really haven't thought about something, *a wise leader doesn't tell them what to do* or tell them the answer ... rather, he or she just *helps them develop and refine their thinking* while still acknowledging their contribution. After all, the last thing you want to have happen, Robert, is for your people to be afraid to give you their ideas. And they will if you make them feel badly for doing so … and especially for ideas and suggestions that you don't initially understand. So, when this happens just say, '*Thank you for telling me that or for suggesting that.*' But I also need you to think a bit more on some of the problems that we discussed. Please get back to me when you have done so. But, thanks once again for the discussion. I enjoyed it.'

"I have to tell you, though, Robert," the wise old man continued, "I've sometimes been amazed at how deep a team member's thinking has gone regarding a particular problem for which I've asked an opinion. My probing questions have actually caused me to reconsider my original thoughts. And guess what, I never had to reveal that it was me holding the 'dumb solution'. So, **MY** questions and **THEIR** great answers allowed me to test the logic behind my own solution. And, together, **WE** have developed many great solutions. So, then, we **ALL** get to 'feel good' about ourselves."

Philip suddenly reached into his desk drawer and handed Robert a sheet of paper. "Here, Robert," he said, "here's my list of questions that I've collected over the years that I think make a difference in how a leader operates. I use this list to remind myself about the important questions that I need to keep asking my team members." It read:

IMPORTANT QUESTIONS
WISE LEADERS ASK OFTEN

What do you think/recommend?

Do you have any ideas or suggestions on ...?

How might we possibly ...?

What's preventing us from ...?

What's holding us back ...?

Why do you think/feel this way?

Is there a better way?

What do you like most/least about us/our Agency/
our company/your job?

What would you change if you could?

Why are you/we doing this?

Why are you/we doing this in this manner?

What do you want from this Agency/job?

What should we stop doing/start doing?

Philip looked at his watch. It was nearing noon and he had a lunch appointment to keep. He got up, put on his jacket and started walking towards the door. As he did so he said, "You know, Robert, it's a funny business being a leader. You start out thinking that you are supposed to have all of the answers and you wind up realizing that you don't have that many ... and too few good ones. But, a wise leader remembers the old adage that *'none of us is as smart as all of us'* and that his job is *to tap the creative and intellectual capital of all his people.* There's gold locked inside the heads of Michael and Susan. Go dig for it, Robert! They already know what they need to do. They already understand the mission statement's message. They just need your help in articulating and expressing those ideas."

'Thanks Philip," said Robert. "any other advice?"

"Sure...lots," the wise old man smiled, "but, for now, let me just add one thing. Whatever ideas or suggestions the three of you come up with - and eventually all agree upon - *you must make sure that they are very specific and measurable so that there is no confusion as to what anything means.* You want to be able to know whether their ideas are being implemented. You want to be able to see what they say they are going to do and to know whether or not it has been done."

Robert followed Philip out to the parking lot. The

two men said good-bye to each other with Philip again offering to see Robert should he need to carry on their discussion.

Robert said, "No, Philip, I think I now know what I need to do and," he paused, "I guess so do Michael and Susan also … I just never realized it. Thanks Philip." With that, Robert turned away and walked towards his car to plan his afternoon with his two team members.

After lunch, Robert found Michael and Susan at their work stations and asked them if they wouldn't mind staying after work "for no more than thirty minutes" to discuss some issues that concerned him. Both agreed. He also made a call to the company's head office to organize a survey of expectations that his Agency's clients might have when telephoning into his Agency. Unfortunately, he was told that the survey and report containing the results would take about two months. "Philip was right again." thought Robert to himself and so he started to formulate his own action plan for understanding - and delivering - what his clients might want.

When it was 'quitting time', and the Agency's telephones were forwarded to the after-hours call center, Robert brought both team members into his office and said, "Thanks for agreeing to stay a few minutes extra, folks. I need your help."

"That's okay, Robert." interjected Susan. "We're happy to help you in any way that we can. What's up?"

Robert began, "I'm a bit concerned, Susan. You see, I believe that you both know the company's new mission statement."

"Absolutely," Michael exclaimed, "how could we not know it with everything that you've put us through to learn it? My wife said that I even mumbled it in my sleep the other night".

They all laughed. Robert continued, "That's great, Michael! But, I've been thinking an awful lot about what we've been doing and I've come to the conclusion that it's just not enough to know and remember an important message like the mission statement. It's also important *to understand what the mission statement message means at a very personal level.* We have to know and understand *what the mission statement message means in terms of how we do our individual jobs.* Otherwise, it's just a bunch of words on a piece of paper and no one will really know what to do with it."

"I'm not sure that I buy what you're saying," said Michael, a bit disapprovingly.

"Why?" Robert replied.

"Because our mission statement says that we will 'provide insurance products of the highest quality and service'. Our mission statement has nothing to do with me or Susan. It emphasizes the company's products. So the people most affected by the new mission statement are really the folks who design our products at company's head office and those in our Agency responsible for selling our products in the field ... not a couple of telephone jockeys like us. Aren't I right, Susan?"

Susan was silent.

"I see," said Robert. "I now have a clearer picture of why you feel the way that you do and ... by the way, thank you for telling me that. But, are you absolutely sure that the mission statement message, and I mean the whole mission statement message, has nothing to do with us?

"Remember, it says, 'Our mission is to provide insurance products of the highest quality and service that will truly delight and amaze each and every client that we are privileged to serve.' *Surely, there is some way that we can take those words, or even some of those words, and make them apply to us.* What do you think?"

After a few moments of silence, Susan piped up, "Well, I suppose the words 'delight and amaze each and every client' could apply to my job."

"You know, Susan, I think you're right!" replied an excited Robert. And at that he took two pads of paper that were on his desk and handed one each to Michael and Susan. Robert then said, "Look guys. Please just humor and bear with me for a moment. But would you quickly jot down any ideas or suggestions that you have in terms of how you might, as part of your telephone responsibilities on the team, 'truly delight and amaze each and every one of our clients?'"

And remembering how Philip had done it with him, Robert added, "... and please don't pre-judge or over analyze your answers. Just write down quickly whatever comes into your head ... and I'm going to do the exercise as well."

After a few minutes had passed, Robert asked Michael and Susan to each read their answers out loud while he recorded them on the flip chart beside his desk. He read his own list last. To everyone's amazement, Robert's list was the shortest and really didn't add anything extra. The summary of their responses looked as follows:

Michael's and Susan's Suggestions on How They Might, as Part of Their Telephone Responsibilities, *'Truly Delight and Amaze Each and Every One of Our Clients'*

1. Answer the phone very quickly when it rings.
   ***

2. Answer with a very friendly and inviting greeting. ***

3. Answer with a very warm and friendly tone of voice and maintain it throughout the call. ***

4. Ask for the caller's name early and repeat it back many times throughout the call. *

5. Never say "NO" to a caller.*

6. Sincerely apologize for having to put a caller "ON HOLD". **

7. Always thank the caller for calling. **

8. When ending a call - or transferring a call - do so with a sincere expression of appreciation. *

*'s = number of people mentioning the item

All three eventually decided that they should combine items 7 & 8.

"What a fantastic list of ideas!" exclaimed Robert with a broad grin. "Which ones do you think that we should do?"

"All of them," proclaimed Susan enthusiastically.

"I agree," said Michael, a little more subdued, however.

"Do you really think that you can do all of them?" asked Robert.

"Absolutely!" Susan almost shouted.

Robert then thought of Philip's parting advice and said, "But, don't you think we also need to be a bit more specific for some of these?"

"What do you mean?" asked Susan.

"I mean that I think that we **should specify and agree on what it means 'to answer the phone quickly' so that there is no confusion.** In other words, how many rings should the caller hear before we should answer?"

After a brief discussion, they all agreed that they should set the target number of rings - the standard - at two. They also agreed that they should try to say a caller's name a minimum of three times during the conversation.

"And what about the greetings?" Robert added. "Do you think that *we should specify and agree on* the words in the initial telephone greeting as well as in the closing expression of appreciation?"

Both Michael and Susan seemed to chime "yes" together.

Robert then asked them to again use their pads and individually write out a proposed greeting and expression of appreciation that they might both eventually agree to use. Robert also wrote out a proposed greeting and 'expression' for himself. When they were finished, he wrote out the suggestions that each team member had on the flip chart *(revealing his own version last)* and together they 'massaged' the words into a final format.

The initial telephone greeting and expression of appreciation that they eventually agreed upon went as follows:

INITIAL TELEPHONE GREETING:

Good day and welcome to Robert Craig's Insurance and Financial Services Agency. This is Michael/Susan. To whom do I have the pleasure of speaking?

Person responds with their name - or not.

Then, we say:

Thank you for calling our Agency, (add person' s name- if available). How may I help you?

Then, say the person's name as frequently as possible (minimum three times during the conversation).

****

EXPRESSION OF APOLOGY FOR PUTTING A CALLER ON HOLD.

I am very sorry (Say name) and please excuse me, but I need to put you 'on hold' for a moment. I promise to get back to you very quickly, thank you. And, once again, my apologies.

****

EXPRESSION OF APPRECIATION AT THE END OF EVERY CALL (or when transferring a call):

Thank you for calling Robert Craig's Insurance and

Financial Services Agency (say person's name) and it's been a pleasure speaking with you today.

When they were done, Robert surveyed the list of suggestions that they had created and said, "Wow, I would think that any caller would be both delighted and amazed if you gave them everything on that list. Now, are you guys really sure that you can do all of them? Have we created something here that is realistic and doable?"

Both Michael and Susan expressed their agreement. They also vowed to each other that starting tomorrow, they would begin implementing all of the ideas that they had generated that afternoon. Susan even said that she would arrange to have formal printed copies of their ideas prepared and distributed. They then all gave each other 'high five' hand slaps and words of congratulation.

Because it was getting late Robert told them to 'call it a day'. As Michael and Susan left his office, Robert beamed with delight. "Well," he thought, "they finally **know what to do!**"

The Second Question

The next several days proved to be extremely busy ones for Robert. It was the third quarter in his agency's fiscal year and Robert's annual planning cycle was in high gear. He was analyzing the monthly Quality and Production Reports to ensure that he was attaining his sales goals. Robert wondered how he was going to get all of his "client field work" AND "desk work" done. So, he worked late into the evening most nights and came to work early every morning. Robert loved being an agent and all of the responsibilities associated with owning his own business. He would not allow himself to fail.

Michael's and Susan's development was always on his mind though. He wanted to ensure their success and improve the quality of his Agency team's results. Using a feature of the office's telephone system, he occasionally listened in on Michael's and Susan's telephone calls. A couple of times, he disguised his voice and phoned into the Agency. He also stood nonchalantly outside Michael and Susan's work stations to see how they were interacting with the Agency's clients.

Unfortunately, Robert was not as pleased as he wanted to be with their progress. While he wanted to give them time to adjust their behaviors to the new agreed upon "standards" – standards that they had helped create – he felt that little to no effort was being put into their implementation. For instance, it was only once that Robert observed the phone being answered on the second ring. Most of the time, it was five, six or even seven rings - and sometimes even longer.

It was Robert's impression that these situations occurred because Michael and Susan would either be in the middle of a conversation that they did not wish to interrupt or doing other work from which they did not want to pull themselves away immediately. He also witnessed several occasions in which courier drivers appeared to receive more attention from the two team members than their ringing phones.

As for their other '*Mission Statement Task List*' items, Robert observed that while Susan appeared to be trying to use the various telephone greetings and expressions, Michael, on the other hand, never did. Both Michael and Susan also seemed to say "NO" a lot to their callers. And, as for both team members' 'tone of voice', it was, in Robert's opinion neither warm nor friendly. "They sound like barking dogs." thought Robert. "So, why aren't they doing what the mission statement needs them to do?...and what they agreed to do?"

Robert then remembered Philip's famous first question to him: "**Do they know what to do?**" So he decided to test this for himself. He asked both Michael and Susan if they knew the mission statement. They claimed that they did and when he asked them to recite it, they did so effortlessly. Robert then asked them if they knew what the mission statement meant in terms of their jobs. It was here that Robert discovered a problem.

To his dismay, both Michael and Susan could only vaguely remember the tasks from the 'Mission Statement Task List' that they had generated and agreed to follow just two weeks before. "Holy cow," thought Robert, "they still really don't *know what to do*. Being an agent is a lot tougher than I had thought it would be."

Robert, however, was better prepared this time. He told Michael and Susan that he was disappointed in their knowledge of the Mission Statement Task List; that he was going to treat it in the same way that he had dealt with the mission statement; and, that he expected them both to memorize it and to be able to recite it. "After all," said the clever young man to both of them, "if you can't say it, you can't live it, right?" Both Michael and Susan agreed with this and promised to memorize the "MSTL" (Susan's new name for the Mission Statement Task List).

Over the next week, Robert took Michael and Susan each morning through a sort of 'morning roll call' on the mission statement and MSTL. The first few days met with some mild resistance. But Robert was determined and he told both Michael and Susan that he was going to *relentlessly make them repeat the list over and over again* until they succeeded.

And in a short while they did. "We were cajoled into submission." Susan told her lunch mates in the local mall's food court one day.

"Ahhh," thought Robert rather confidently, "now they really *know what to do.*" But, he was soon to be disappointed again. His subsequent informal checks on how well Michael and Susan were performing the Mission Statement Task List showed that nothing had actually changed. "They *know what to do,*" Robert said to himself "however, they are still not doing what I need them to do...what they agreed to do." Robert was dejected. As a result, he was becoming very frustrated with the entire process of leading his team.

As luck would have it, though, Robert found himself at a breakfast meeting the next day in which the wise old man was present. As the meeting ended, Philip asked Robert, "So, my clever young man, how are things going with Michael and Susan?"

"I'm afraid that they're still not doing what needs to be done." he said.

"But, *do they know what to do?*" asked the wise old man.

"Yes." said Robert, "they absolutely *know what to do.* There is no doubt in my mind." And he then recounted for Philip all of his efforts to translate the mission statement message. He recounted the Mission Statement Task List that Michael and Susan had both generated, agreed to and memorized.

"Okay, it sounds like they both know what to do. But, *do they know why they should be doing these things?*" retorted the wise old man.

"Do they know why they should be doing these things?" repeated Robert with an incredulous tone in his voice. "I should certainly hope so."

"Well, you'd better make sure," replied Philip, "because *when people understand 'the why' about something that they have to do, they tend to work at it more than when they don't.* If Michael and Susan don't understand 'the why', it will be a lot harder for them to accept the new tasks on the Mission Statement Task List. So, if I were you, I would make sure that they both *know why they need to do what they agreed to do.*"

The two men parted, leaving Robert to reflect on the wise old man's latest question.

Since Robert was swamped with his own work, he decided to wait a few days before he spoke with Michael and Susan. He would use the time to collect his thoughts on what he wanted to say to them. But, he also wanted to conduct his own informal survey of telephone callers, telling them about the Agency's mission statement and asking them for ideas on how his Agency might live up to its promise to 'delight and amaze' them when they phoned in. If no suggestions were immediately forthcoming, Robert would prompt them by going over the Mission Statement Task List and asking their opinion about each item. To his utter surprise, no new items were introduced. Interestingly, most thought that the idea of 'never saying no' was silly and impractical.

About ten days later, Robert asked his two Client Care team members to come in a bit early so that they could "talk about some things". He even arranged to have a light breakfast ready for them when they arrived. But, Robert also remembered some of the wise old man's earlier advice about what everyone wants: **to feel good about themselves, to feel that what they do matters and to feel 'respected, and appreciated'**, just like the mission statement says. And so he began, "First of all let me say that I have really appreciated all the support that you have given me in some of the initiatives that I have tried to institute since taking over this Agency. I know that sometimes, it's probably not been easy working with me. You're the first people that I have ever had to manage and so I know that I'm probably making a lot of mistakes. However, I want to thank you for your patience with me. I have to tell you, though, I'm having to learn a lot of stuff really quickly and I hope you know how much I will continue to need your help and advice as we go along."

"We do, Robert," said Susan, "and, thank you for telling us this."

"I also have some interesting information to share with you" continued Robert and he then proceeded to tell them about the results of his informal survey of client needs. "So you see folks," he said, "I think my survey shows that we were able to second guess our clients' needs fairly well ... and, so, congratulations. However, given the responses I received concerning the 'never say no' idea from the Mission Statement Task List, what do you think we should do?"

After some humorous conversation around this particular item, Michael recommended that they drop that item from the MSTL. Susan echoed her support for Michael's recommendation with the words, "I second the motion!"

"Okay," said Robert, "I concur ... But, I also have a problem." Robert paused for effect. "I know that both you guys know what this Agency needs you to do in your job ... at least insofar as your telephone responsibilities are concerned. You both know the mission statement ... right?"

"We sure do." replied Michael.

"And you both now can recite the Mission Statement Task List that you both agreed you'd do ... don't you?

"Right again," answered Susan.

"Then, for Pete's sake, why the heck aren't you guys doing these things?" asked a frustrated Robert.

He then told them how his informal checks revealed that there were problems in implementing all of the new changes that they had agreed to.

Turning specifically to Michael, Robert said, "And you, Michael ... you seem to be having more problems than Susan ... why? Why are you not doing what you agreed to do? Please tell me so that I can at least understand."

"Well, if you must know," Michael stammered, "I find that I feel kind of silly doing these things. I know that you spent some time explaining how we could make a connection or link between our jobs in answering the telephone and the new mission statement. But, I still don't see why we have to do this.

All mission statements are just a load of B.S. anyway and it seems to me that you're just forcing us to do something that really doesn't matter.... that won't make a difference one way or the other. And, as I said before, I really think the new mission statement, if it means anything, is intended more for the guys at the head office and for the sales part of our Agency; not for the kind of routine 'admin/client service jobs' that we do here. Right, Susan?"

"I hate to admit it, Robert," Susan replied, "but I kind of agree with Michael. I really don't feel comfortable doing many of the things on our Mission Statement Task List and they seem a bit forced, if you know what I mean. So, like Michael, *I just don't see the need for doing them.*"

Robert was completely taken aback and thought, "The wise old man was right, they don't know **why** they should be doing what the company and my Agency need them to do." He then said, "Well, this has come as quite a surprise to me guys. But, thank you for your honesty and trust. Thank you for telling me how you both feel. Now let me ask you something." Robert paused, "Can you please tell me why a business exists?"

"Sure...that's easy," laughed Michael. "To make money."

"And you're absolutely right," replied Robert. "If a

business does not make any money it will not exist. It will not survive. It will not have the profits either to re-invest into itself or to provide a return on investment to the owners. But what I want you to tell me is what every business has to do *to come into existence*. What is it that every business must do, at the beginning, in order to exist ... and if it fails to do that consistently, it will not exist?"

"That's easy too," answered Susan, "a business exists because it's able to satisfy a need."

"Right again," Robert proclaimed excitedly, "a business comes into existence   because it is able to satisfy someone's needs. If a business is not able to satisfy - and continue to satisfy - the needs of its clients, it will not only fail to retain these clients, it will also fail to attract new ones. And if this happens, the business will eventually fail to exist. So, satisfying clients' needs is pretty important, wouldn't you say?"

Both Michael and Susan murmured their agreement.

"And that's why we have the mission statement." Robert continued. "The mission statement is there to communicate to all of us - me, the Agent, and you, my team members - it is what we currently **need to** *focus on* in order to exist ... in other words, to attract, win and retain clients.

"While the mission statement tells us what we need to do, it also captures the spirit and attitude we need to have in order for us to make the mission a reality."

"Okay," said Michael, "but, like I said before, what's that got to do with me ... or Susan and our jobs at your Agency?"

"Absolutely everything!" said Robert emphatically. "Don't you see, Michael, we're not the only game in town, right? We live in a competitive world. Our clients have many choices regarding with whom they decide to do business. It's kind of like always living in the 'singles scene'... we never really marry any of our clients, we just date them ... and we want our clients to keep dating us forever. Which brings me to my next question: How do you think our clients go about deciding which insurance Agency is right for them...? Which Agency to date?"

Susan grinned at the analogy and said, "Probably, the one that always makes sure that they have a good experience ... and the one that satisfies their overall needs the best. Otherwise, you would probably decline going on a second date."

"Right on!" Robert responded. "And that's why our mission statement doesn't just simply say that we want to satisfy our clients, but rather that we want to 'truly delight and amaze' them. Now, how do you think we might go about proving to a client that we are serious about what we are saying ... that we are telling the truth in our mission statement and not just promoting some clever sounding phrases or slogans when we want to feel better about ourselves as an organization?"

"That's easy to answer," said Susan. "A client can tell by the way the business treats them ... and especially by the way that the team members in that business act and respond to their needs."

"I agree with you one hundred per cent", Robert replied enthusiastically. "*Actions speak louder than words.* It's a notion that has been around for a very long time. In fact, you can even find references to it in the Bible.

"Amen," Susan rejoined emphatically.

Robert smiled. Michael, on the other hand, appeared glum.

Turning to him directly, Robert said, "Michael, our mission statement is our statement of faith. But for the mission statement to come alive, to be more than just a set of nice sounding words, *we have to live the mission and to make it part of our everyday activities.* That's why we had to break down the mission statement and translate it so that it could be understood and practiced by every team member.

"But, if we are going to 'truly delight and amaze' each and every client all the time, as our mission says, *it's not just enough for one or two people in our Agency to live the mission. We all have to.* And that's why it's important for every person in the Agency to do their part in helping to make the mission statement come alive. Do you see what I'm saying?"

"I think I'm beginning to see what you mean." said Michael softly.

"Let me now show you something else to help reinforce my point," continued Robert and he got up and walked over to his flip chart. He then drew the following sketch on the top page and said, "Michael, I want you to imagine that this is a picture of a beach, with a bunch of seagulls resting quietly on the shore.

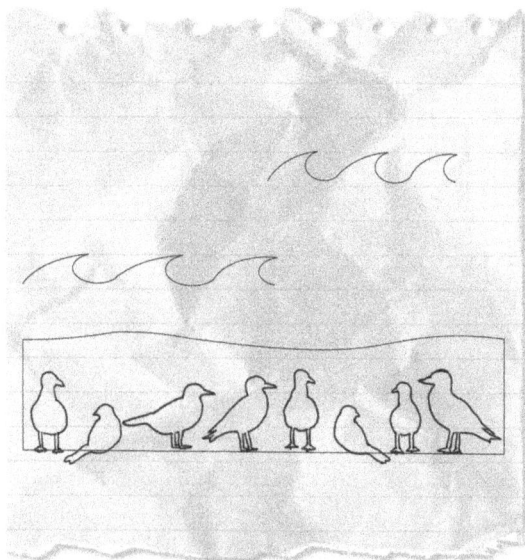

Now imagine what would happen if a big dog were suddenly to emerge and, upon seeing the seagulls, it decided to charge the resting flock of birds. What do you think would happen? Describe the picture that you would see." Robert asked.

"There'd be chaos," said Michael.

"Definitely!" smiled Robert and he then proceeded to complete his picture with wild strokes.

Robert flipped the page over and drew the first picture again. He then said, "Okay, now I want you to imagine the same beach ... only this time it has a different set of birds on it ... they're called Canadian Geese. Have you ever seen one?"

"Yeah," Susan blurted out. "They're pretty big birds with ... kind of fat bodies. Grey in color, I think."

"That's pretty close," said Robert. "As a matter of fact, the birds are really heavy. But the remarkable thing about them is that each year, they make a journey with a round-trip distance of approximately eight thousand miles. In the fall, they travel from their home in Canada to spend the winter in Mexico ... and then return back to Canada in the spring. It's an incredible journey. Now, many people have speculated as to what could possibly enable such birds - birds that look 'aerodynamically challenged' - to accomplish such a feat. It is generally believed that it has a lot to do with how they fly together."

Robert poised his flip chart pen at the ready and said, "So imagine that we are on that same beach, but with the Canadian Geese there this time and the same dog comes along and charges them. Could either one of you describe for me what the picture would look like after a few minutes?"

Both Michael and Susan remained silent.

Robert responded for them. "The birds would quickly adopt a flying formation that would look something like this." He then proceeded to make the following sketch ...

"They would create this 'V' formation," Robert continued, "which, incidentally, is how you can always recognize Canadian Geese when you see them in flight ... especially during their migration season. However, it is also believed that flying in this 'V' formation is the most important factor that makes it possible for these birds to complete their annual journey so efficiently. You see, the lead bird has the primary responsibility for setting the direction for the flock and for navigation. The only problem is that the lead bird takes the full brunt of the wind's force and tires very quickly. When this happens a special maneuver takes place in which the lead bird rotates to the back of the flock's 'V' formation and the next bird in line takes over 'flying point'.

"Now, what's so special about rotating to the back position, you ask? The theory goes that as each bird flaps its huge wings, it creates a minor up-draft, or up-lift, for the birds following behind ... and that the effect is cumulative. In other words, the strongest uplift from all the birds flapping their wings is felt at the very back - which just happens to be the place where the bird that is most tired goes to recuperate after having flown point.

"It is believed that the net result of this particular flying formation and rotation maneuver is that the entire flock is able to cover a significantly greater flying distance each day, and far more efficiently, than if each bird was trying to make the journey on its own.

"But the key to the birds' success lies in the fact that each bird instinctively knows what it must do to help the whole flock accomplish its mission. Each bird knows and understands the importance of *staying in formation* and each bird *knows the important role that it plays - whatever its position - in terms of helping the entire flock achieve its goals both more effectively and efficiently."*

"See this bird, here," Robert said as he pointed emphatically to one of the middle circles that he had drawn in the 'V' formation. "This bird does not say to itself, 'What I do doesn't matter.' It doesn't say, 'No one really cares whether I stay in formation or not.' Instead, it knows that what it does, no matter how small it may seem to be, contributes to the success of the flock and that if it were to break formation, it could jeopardize the entire organization."

"And so, I guess what I am trying to emphasize here for you Michael - and for you too Susan - is that what you do in your jobs at this Agency matters an awful lot in terms of achieving our mission. You both have a vital and important role to play in your jobs here in terms of helping to make the mission statement come alive, satisfying our clients and making the Agency successful. After all, you're usually the first people that clients have contact with when they phone our Agency. You're their first experience with our mission. If clients get 'turned-off' based on how you treat them when they phone us, they may decide that they don't want to do business with us. And so, we all have a part to play, guys, when it comes to making the mission real. If we are really going to become an Agency that 'truly delights and amazes' our client then it's going to require a contribution from each and every one of us. Not just from some of us, but from all of us ... and all of the time. Do you see what

I mean?'"

"I had never really thought about it that way," said Michael.

"That's okay," said Robert. "I'm just sorry that we didn't have this conversation earlier. It might have made things a lot easier in terms of **knowing why** I was doing some of the things that I did ... and **knowing why** I needed you to do certain things in a certain way. I'm sorry for not explaining '*the why*' better.

"But now also know this," continued Robert. "I really do value what you and Susan are doing and I continue to need your help if we are going to become a mission driven Agency - one that truly delights and amazes each and every client. Can I count on you?"

"You can count on us, right Michael," said Susan.
"You betcha!" Michael responded.

"Yikes! Look at the time!" exclaimed Susan. "We've got about sixty seconds to open the Agency's telephone lines. We'd better get going, Robert, or we will wind up amazing our clients the wrong way for sure."

Robert laughed. "Okay," he said, "and once again folks, thanks for coming in early." Michael and Susan then made a dash for Robert's office door.

Robert was pleased. "*They know what to do,*" he thought, rather contentedly. "*And they now know why they should do it. So now, they should start doing what this Agency needs them to do* ...what they agreed to do".

Later in the morning, Susan came to Robert's office during her break and dropped off some summary notes that she thought would help her remember some of the ideas that Robert had passed on to her. Robert's spirits soared as he reviewed Susan's handiwork. It read:

Making Our Mission Statement Come Alive

The primary mission of every business is to satisfy the needs of its clients.

The business that satisfies its clients the best, wins.

Talk is cheap. We must show our clients that we love them. Actions speak louder than words.

Satisfying clients is the responsibility of every team member.

I can make a difference by how I personally act. I can make a contribution to the implementation of the mission and the success of the Agency in my job.

STAY IN FORMATION!

The Third Question

As the days passed, Robert tried to find as many opportunities as possible to see how Michael and Susan were doing. He continued to ask them to recite the mission statement and their Mission Statement Task List every few days. He was delighted that they both continued to excel in this area. Robert was also very pleased to find that both Michael and Susan seemed to say the new greeting and expression of appreciation during each call without exception and with ease. It was his perception, however, that problems continued to exist in terms of answering the phone within two rings and always repeating the client's name during their conversations. He also thought that Susan seemed to be putting more effort into these tasks than Michael.

The problem area that concerned Robert the most, though, was the tone of voice that each person used in speaking to the callers. Robert thought that their voices "sounded a bit grating", as he put it and "not nearly warm and friendly enough". "I wonder if they still don't *know what to do* on this one," he thought to himself. Robert, therefore, decided to speak to both team members about this issue one morning in his office before they opened the phone lines.

****

"What do you mean, 'I have a problem with the way that you're speaking to the clients?'" asked Michael, a bit annoyed. "What's wrong now? Aren't we saying the right words that you wanted us to?"

Robert could sense that he had entered into a touchy area. "Yes," he replied, "you're saying the right words alright, but not the way that this Agency needs you to say them. It's really more about the tone of voice that you use."

"Our tone of voice?" Susan asked with a perplexed expression on her face. "What's wrong with our tone of voice?"

"Well," replied Robert. "It's my impression that you guys are not being very warm and friendly with the tone of voice that you are using when speaking to callers. Oh sure, you say all the right words that we agreed to … but, it seems to me that the tone you're using is much too flat. It just doesn't seem friendly and inviting enough. In fact when I've listened to some of your telephone conversations, it almost seems as though you are speaking with people that our Agency has never met before and who do not have a relationship with us. This is really counterproductive because our sales team sells on relationship, not on price. I need you to continue to further develop the relationship that our sales team started … or put another way, ask yourselves how you would like to be greeted by a person you have been dating?"

"I'm not really sure what you mean," said Michael with a stressed look on his face. He was clearly growing impatient.

"I thought you might say that," Robert rejoined, "so, I did some research and found the telephone numbers of three companies whose team members, in my opinion, answer the phone with a very warm and friendly tone. But first let me play for you a recording of how the two of you sound to a caller."

Michael and Susan were taken aback that Robert had the ability to record their conversations.

It was Michael's voice that they heard first giving the agreed-upon greeting. It blared out over the speakerphone. Then it was Susan's turn. Both agreed that that was how they typically sounded when they answered the phone.

Robert then dialed the first of the telephone numbers that he wanted to use as role models. The difference from how Michael and Susan answered the phone was startling. While the words used to greet the callers were not as compelling as the ones that they had crafted, the telephone operator's voice itself was, as Susan put it, 'silky smooth'.

The next two examples were equally instructive. And in between each call, Robert played the recording that he had made of Michael and Susan to further highlight and reinforce the differences with the way that they spoke.

"Now do you *see* what I mean?" asked Robert.

Michael grew flushed and seemed ready to explode. "Listen here, Robert." he said with a strained voice. "This is the only voice that I've got and I have used it my whole life. It hasn't caused me any trouble up until now and, quite frankly, sir, you seem to be the only person that has a problem with it."

Robert remained calm. He knew that he was at a critical point with Michael. He responded quietly. "Please, Michael, I am not trying to upset you," He paused, "... and please forgive me if I am doing so. It's just that you both agreed a while back ... when we put the mission statement task list together ... remember? ... that we should always try to answer the phone with a warm and friendly tone of voice ... isn't that what we agreed?"

Both Michael and Susan remained silent.

Eventually Robert asked, "And why are we doing this?"

"To delight and amaze our clients." said Susan, jumping in.

"That's right," Robert smiled. "So, the only thing that I am doing here, right now, is trying to give you guys some feedback on this one area and to give you a better idea of what you need to do when a client calls our Agency. We should always be answering with a warm and friendly tone of voice in order to 'delight and amaze' our clients as our mission statement says we must do."

"You're both progressing well. You're doing a great job with the greetings and I really appreciate that you are saying them so diligently. I just think that you need to work a little harder and concentrate more on how you say those words ... Okay? As a matter of fact, let me give you my own version of what I think it means to answer the phone with a warm and friendly voice."

And at that, Robert picked up his telephone and pretended that a caller was phoning the Agency.

"Good afternoooooon and welcome to Robert Craig's Insurance and Financial Services Agency," he purred. "This is Robert," he said, almost breathlessly. "To whom do I have the pleasure of speaking?" Robert's voice was now an incredibly pleasant mixture of soft yet varied tones. It was definitely not Robert's usual speaking voice though. He then went on to repeat the simulated caller's name four times. He pretended to put the caller on hold and then signed-off with the agreed upon expression. His execution of the scripted words was flawless.

When he was finished with his mock call, Robert looked at Michael and Susan and said, "There ... now do you have a clearer picture of what I am talking about? Do you *see* what I am saying?"

"And you expect us to do that?" asked Michael with a hint of skepticism in his voice.

"Absolutely," Robert replied. "and do you know why?"

"I suppose so," said Michael.

"No, Michael," came Robert's swift rebuttal. "Don't suppose. Know! Tell me why we need to do things the way that we said ... the way that we specified in the mission task list. Prove to me that you know **why** we are doing what we are doing."

Michael stumbled though his response. But, he still managed to cover the main points of Robert's earlier speech about satisfying the client and satisfying the client better than the competition.

Robert was pleased. "At least he knows 'the why'," he thought to himself. "Look folks," he continued aloud, "I've tried to show you how other companies are doing it. I've even shown you that I can do it.... And if I can do this, so can you. So please, give it another try. Try to be warmer and more friendly. I know that you both can do this if you want to ... alright?"

"Okay," said Susan, "I'll try my best!"

"Sure, Robert," responded Michael. But it was Robert's impression as Michael left his office that his response sounded less than whole-hearted.

Over the next few days, Robert tried to observe if there were any noticeable changes in the way that Michael and Susan spoke to their callers. Susan took up the challenge right away. But Robert became concerned when it appeared that Susan was experimenting with a variety of different voices. Susan seemed to be losing the confidence that Robert used to sense in her when answering the phone prior to their last meeting. Michael, on the other hand, seemed to have tried at first, but quickly gave up. Robert grew despondent as he realized that he had reached yet another stumbling block with his two Client Care team members.

What to do? As he had not spoken with his old mentor in a while, Robert decided once again to give Philip a call to see what advice the wise old man might have for him. Philip, as usual, expressed that he was glad to hear from the clever young man he admired so much. He suggested that they meet for lunch the next day.

As they sat down at their table in a popular local restaurant Philip asked, "So, Robert, how goes the battle?"

"Not very well," he replied. "I'm still having problems with Michael and Susan".

"*Do they know what to do?*" asked the wise old

man.

"Undeniably," Robert responded. "They know the mission statement. They understand the mission statement. And they know what they specifically have to do to make a contribution to the mission statement in their jobs. I know this for sure."

"*And do they know why they need to do it?*" pressed the wise old man.

"Without a doubt," said Robert. "I have spent a lot of time explaining *'the why'* to them and I know that they both understand the role that they have to play in making the mission statement a reality." Robert then recounted for the wise old man all of the stories and anecdotes that he had shared with his two client care team members. He concluded by saying, "but they're still not doing everything that the mission and my Agency needs them to do." Robert then relayed his frustration over his inability to have Michael and Susan answer the phone with a warm and friendly tone of voice.

"I see," said the wise old man, "but do they know *how* to do what you are asking them to do? *Do they know how to do it?*"

"How to do it?" Robert repeated back. "Absolutely!" He then described how he had shown Michael and

Susan the three role model examples of telephone greetings at other companies. He also told Philip about his own personal demonstration of answering the phone.

When Robert was finished, the wise old man said, "That's very impressive, Robert. But, it seems to me that all you have really done is shown them more 'what to do' stuff and then proved to them that you can do it. Michael and Susan, however, may still not know how to do what it is that you are asking them to do. It's kind of like swimming, Robert. You can have lots of people demonstrate their forward crawl for you and still not really know how to do it yourself. ... As a matter of fact, I'm not sure if I could do what you are asking Michael or Susan to do ... or, do it the right way at least ... and the reason is because I really wouldn't know how to do what you'd be asking me to do."

"I think I'm beginning to see what you mean." said Robert.

"Now," Philip continued, "if I asked you - or told you - to do something that you felt you didn't know **how** to do, what do you think the natural reaction of most people would be?"

"Fear."

"And what do you think Susan and Michael might be afraid of Robert?"

"They could be afraid of a lot of things," Robert answered nervously. "Afraid of failing. Afraid of looking stupid or dumb."

"And why are most people afraid of looking stupid, Robert?" pressed the wise old man.

"Because," said Robert remembering a previous lesson from Philip, "they then **won't feel good about themselves**. They'll feel inadequate."

"So what then do they do, Robert? What action are they most likely to take?"

"Well ... they'll do nothing. They'll just keep on doing what they have done before."

"Exactly!" said Philip pointedly. "Most people are afraid of the things that they haven't done before because it means that they have to leave what I like to call their '*comfort zone of the familiar*' ... the stuff that they already know how to do...the stuff that already makes them feel good about themselves. Sometimes, when you ask them to do something that they don't know how to do, they might even think that you are setting them up for failure ... as a reason to get rid of them ... Or maybe they even tried it once before and they failed and now they are convinced that it can't be done ... that they cannot do it ... And so **you have to help them get past their fears**.

"Remember what I told you earlier, Robert. **A leader helps his team members** ... and one of the most important things that a leader can do is **to help drive out the fear that they have when you ask them to do something new or unfamiliar**. You need to help Michael and Susan by making certain that they *know how to do what you need them to do*. Only then can you really be certain that the reason they are not doing what you want them to do is not because they are afraid of failing ... or because they have convinced themselves that they will fail!"

"But how could they have convinced themselves that they will fail?"

"Let me answer that with an analogy, Robert ... Have you ever wondered why huge circus elephants will stand still while tethered to just a small stake in the ground? As far as you or I are concerned, we know for sure that if the elephant wanted to wander about, that small stake would not be strong enough to hold it in place. So why then doesn't the elephant simply lift its huge foot and go wherever it wants? The answer it seems is that the elephant is somehow convinced that it cannot escape ... that the stake is stronger than it is.

"And, 'Why does the elephant think this way?' you ask? Because when the elephant was a baby, that stake was indeed strong enough. And every time the elephant tried to get away, it found that it could not succeed. So, after many attempts and an equal number of failures, the elephant became convinced that it could not overcome the strength of the stake. Then the elephant grows up. But because of all its past experiences, it never tries to escape because it is convinced that it can't ... so, the elephant doesn't even try ...

"Too often, Robert, people will also act like those circus elephants. Because of 'bad' past experiences, they think 'bad' thoughts about themselves ...there's this little voice inside their heads telling them that they're no good, that they're failures and that they shouldn't even try because they'll fail just like all the other times they tried. Good leaders, however, help to silence that voice and in so doing help their followers to see new possibilities ... the new possibilities of success! In order for that to happen, a good leader makes sure his followers **know how to do what they are being asked to do**. Have I answered your question, Robert?"

"Totally, and once again Philip, you've given me some outstanding advice ... Thank you." Robert said admiringly.

"You're welcome, Robert." Philip warmly responded, "But, remember what Mark Twain once said about advice."

"What's that?"

"That it's better to give than to receive."

The two men laughed at Philip's remark and carried on with their lunch ...

When Robert later returned to his Agency, he asked both Michael and Susan to stay, once again, for a few minutes after work. They both agreed. Robert decided to use part of his afternoon to prepare for his meeting with them. When the appointed time arrived, Michael and Susan strolled into Robert's office together.

"What's up, boss?" Susan chirped and slumped down into one of the chairs beside Robert's desk. Michael decided to remain standing.

"Guys," Robert began, "I'm sorry that I had to ask you to stay late yet again. But, I'm still having a problem with the way that you're both answering the phone ... in particular, with the tone of voice that you're both using."

"Oh, no!" cried Michael. "Not this again. What's wrong with my tone now? You know that I've been trying."

"Yeah," Susan joined in, "me too! As a matter of fact, I'm starting to drive myself crazy with it. Michael says that I am starting to sound like a person with a split personality...Several of them actually."

The three of them laughed.

"Relax folks," Robert said. "I'm here to tell you that I know you've been trying. But I also want to ask you one thing."

"What's that?" the two team members blurted out simultaneously.

"I want to know if you **know how to do** what I am asking you to do?"

"Not really," said Susan, who then added, "or, at least, I'm not sure if I'm doing it the right way ... or at least the way you want me to do it."

"What about you, Michael?" Robert asked.

"Well ...," came his reply. "I know **what** you want me to do and **why** you want me to do it but ... I'm not sure that I can do it. I don't feel really confident."

"I thought so," said Robert. "So I want to take your worries away...for the both of you. I've finally realized that I need to help teach you **how** to do **what** I need you to do." And at that Robert proceeded to tell them that he had arranged for a voice coach to come in for an hour every other afternoon. The coach would work with them individually for about two weeks to help them "smooth out the warbles in their voices".

Both Michael and Susan agreed that such training sessions would probably help a lot in terms of showing them how to regulate the tones in their voices. This training might standardize how they would both speak and give them more confidence when doing their jobs. They ended by thanking Robert 'for not giving up on them'. And with that, Robert told his two team members to hurry home to their families and to keep him informed on how they liked the training.

Robert left his office very happy that evening.

The Fourth Question

The next day, as Robert had promised, the voice coach arrived. At first, he just observed Michael and Susan. Later, he took each person aside into a vacant office and did some facial and neck exercises with them. He taught them how to hold their heads and how to tense certain muscles in their necks and throats. For the next session, he brought in an oscilloscope and used the machine to further instruct the two team members. These sessions continued on for the next two weeks. The results were immediately noticeable ... and dramatic. Both Michael and Susan had altered the tone in their voices. As Robert listened to them answer calls, he felt that the money spent on the voice coach was well worth the final result. The voice coach had done his job.

"Michael and Susan certainly know **how** to answer the phone with a warm and friendly tone now." Robert proudly said to himself.

And so it came as somewhat of a surprise, when Robert listened in on their calls a week later, and found that Michael had basically abandoned his recent voice training and returned to his old way of answering the phone. Susan, on the other hand, appeared to have remained true to the lessons that she had learned. In fact, she seemed to revel in the new voice that she had discovered inside herself. Susan called it her 'stage voice' and she would often amuse her colleagues in the Agency's lunchroom by switching back and forth between the two voices.

Robert, however, considered Susan's changes only to be a partial victory. He was still disturbed by the fact that both team members continued to have problems with answering the phone quickly and continuously repeating a caller's name. In mulling the situation over in his mind, Robert concluded that both Michael and Susan "certainly had to **know how** to do these tasks" but that, for some reason, they were not doing them in the way they had previously agreed.

He decided to speak to Philip yet again...

****

"Do they *know what to do?*" the wise old man asked patiently.

"Yes," replied Robert.

"And, do they *know why they should do it?*"

"Definitely," answered Robert.

"And do they *know how to do it?*"

"Unquestionably," came the response.

"I see," said the wise old man. "but, do they **know**

that they should *care* about doing it?"

"Do they know that they should care?" said an exasperated Robert. "They darn well should care! Look at everything that I have done with them ... the explaining, the repetition, the ongoing coaching and the encouragement ... What more could I possibly do?"

"Well," said the wise old man, "for starters you can make sure that both Michael and Susan know that they are being measured regularly in terms of the tasks that you want them to perform. They should know how well they are performing and they should know that you know too. Otherwise, they might simply think that nobody's watching them and, therefore, that nobody else cares, so why should they? Even worse, they might actually think that they're doing a good job ... after all, who's to disprove them? And so they don't think that there's a need to change their behavior."

"But ... but ... " sputtered Robert, "I already do that. I listen in on their phone calls regularly. From time to time I also stand by their work area to try and overhear them speaking to callers. I sometimes even disguise my voice and make 'fake-calls' into the Agency. I then tell them what I have found out."

"That's fine, Robert," said the wise old man, "but it sounds to me that you're simply acting like a cop hiding in the bushes, waiting to hand out speeding tickets. Let me ask you this," he paused. "Apart from you, how do Michael and Susan know how good a job they are doing? How do they know when they are doing a good job - so that they can keep on doing it - and when they are not - so that they can take corrective action on their own?"

"I'm not sure," said the clever young man, "I suppose that I just rely on them to monitor their own actions when I am not around."

"And you should. But, exactly how are they supposed to do that, especially when they are right in the thick of things?" came Philip's swift reply. "Michael and Susan are still in the stage of learning their new behaviors and so they need continued guidance and more frequent feedback from you.

"Imagine a competitive sport Robert, in which no one on the team - and none of the spectators - knows the score of a game until the very end ... or until a referee simply decides to tell everyone. It would be very hard to play, not much fun to watch and it would be difficult for the fans to decide when to cheer or for the players to change strategy. So you need some kind of mechanism that lets the players - and the referees - know the score as the game proceeds ...

"Now, the same holds true for Michael and Susan. They need to *know on a regular and consistent basis how they are both performing and progressing ... and especially whether they are getting better or worse over time* ... and not just at a particular moment. That way, they can better react to your feedback. They need to receive your feedback in a more timely fashion and not just when it's too late to do anything about it ... when the game is almost over."

"I see," Robert interjected, "and so, if I do what you've just told me, will Michael and Susan start to *care* about what they are doing and what the agency needs them to do?"

"Not always," answered the wise old man.

"What do you mean?" asked Robert with a sense of urgency in his voice.

"I mean that sometimes the feedback you give your team members isn't always enough to *motivate them to really care* ... to do what you and your Agency need them to do. And that's because there's still another reason why they might not care."

"And what's that?"

"It has to do with *consequences*, Robert. For some people, if there are no *personal consequences associated with doing, or not doing, certain assigned tasks and behaviors*, they will not be as committed to doing them as they might otherwise be. So, when this happens to any of your team members, you have to figure out a way to let them know that what they choose to do - or not to do- really m*atters ... and that it matters to them personally ... not just to your Agency or the company.*"

"What kind of consequences?" asked Robert. "Do you mean money?"

"Yes and no," answered the wise old man with a sly grin growing on his face. "There's no doubt that money can be a powerful reward mechanism ... and have a very strong effect when it is withheld. But, there are also other ways to really motivate people. And, the one that I have found to be the most useful for creating positive consequences is personal recognition, - you know, the private and public praisings and tributes, as well as the pins, plaques, trophies, certificates and medals which show someone how much he or she is valued and appreciated by the organization."

"Oh, like the pictures on the wall of some companies honoring their team member of the month?" enquired Robert.

"That's right. But I have to warn you, Robert, that it's also important for any personal recognition to be *sincerely given*. You mustn't create a situation in which it's simply somebody's turn to get his or her picture on the wall. Otherwise the recognition will not have its intended effect."

"I see," acknowledged Robert.

Philip continued, "Robert, it's been my experience that we all really crave personal recognition and that when we don't get the recognition and respect that we feel we deserve, we generally use money to try and compensate for it ... which is quite ironic, don't you think?"

"In what way?" Robert replied.

"It's ironic because there is usually only so much money that an organization has at its disposal to dole out for salary increases and merit bonuses ... whereas personal recognition - in all its forms - costs practically nothing to give, is in almost unlimited supply and yet, seems to be the one thing that most would-be leaders, managers and supervisors are very reluctant to hand out to their team members ... which is unfortunate, because there is almost an infinite variety of ways ... more than you or I could ever think up ... in which you could give someone the personal recognition and respect that they desire ... providing they've earned it."

"This is really good advice, as usual," remarked Robert. "But, why didn't you tell me about this 'caring stuff ' when I first came to see you to discuss my problems with Michael and Susan."

"Because," answered the wise old man, "the leadership problems that you described earlier with Michael and Susan often simply disappear once people *'know what to do'*, *'know why they should do it'* and *'know how to do it'*. Remember what I once told you about what everyone wants from his or her job?

Robert was quick to answer, *"To feel good about themselves and to feel that what they do matters and contributes to the success of the organization."*

"Exactly," said Philip. "Well, when your team members know *'the what'* and *'the how'* of their job, they will usually do what you ask them to do because you've helped them feel both competent and confident in doing it. In other words, they feel good about themselves. And once they know *'the why'*, they can also feel good about themselves because they know that what they are doing counts ... that it makes a difference ... and they can see the role that they have to play in helping the entire Agency succeed. Best of all, once all these pieces are in place, team members will usually find or invent their own rewards for doing what you need them to do."

"Come to think of it," Robert interrupted. "Susan does seem to enjoy entertaining clients with her new found ability to switch to her stage voice ... She's found her own positive consequence from the voice change ... Once she knew how to do it."

"Absolutely!" bellowed the wise old man. "However, when you find yourself at a point where *'the what'*, *'the why' and 'the how'* are all in place and you're still not getting the behaviors and actions from your team members that you, as their leader, want and need, you shouldn't despair because your efforts haven't been wasted. That's because you need to have *'the what'*, *'the why' and 'the how'* in place first before you can start setting up mechanisms to help them realize that they should *care*. Otherwise, you're just setting them up to fail."

"To fail?" Robert asked.

"Yes, to fail, Robert," Philip paused. "Think about it. How would you like to have a job in which your boss told you there'd be a reward for doing something, but you didn't understand exactly what it was that he wanted you to do ... and he wouldn't tell you either. Or, how would you like to work for someone who told you there'd be a consequence for not doing something properly, but you didn't know how to do it right and no one would show you? *A leader has to make sure that his team members know 'the what', 'the why' and 'the how' first.* Only when these are in place can he start setting-up the *measurement systems and consequences* that make them know that they **should care**."

At that moment, Philip's assistant knocked gently on the door and informed him that his four o'clock appointment had arrived. Philip looked at Robert and apologized for having to cut their conversation short. Philip then quickly left the room through a side door, leaving Robert in his chair to contemplate everything that Philip had just told him.

Several days passed as Robert thought through his plans to help Michael and Susan *care about what they were doing*. His thinking, however, was interrupted by some encouraging news. The latest Client Telephone Quality Report showed that, for the first time, Robert's clients were no longer generally "dissatisfied" with their telephone experience when calling his Agency. Instead the average rating received for his organization was now in the "satisfied" range.

While Robert knew that he was still not at the level of "delighting and amazing" clients, he felt that the latest survey results provided some vindication and verification of the actions that Michael and Susan were taking.

When he felt that he was finally ready with his plans, Robert called both team members into work early one morning. He began the session by having all three of them *recite in unison the mission statement and the mission statement task list* that they had developed so long ago. When they were done, Robert invited them to "dig in" to the food that he had brought specially for the meeting ... coffee and chocolate glazed donuts for Susan ... coffee and two pineapple danishes for Michael. Because Robert had a tendency to over-order, Susan nicknamed these gatherings as 'Robert's Breakfast Beefings.' But, Susan's label also signified the real purpose of the gathering ... to discuss something that was on Robert's mind.

After some light conversation around current events, Susan resorted to her new "stage voice" and crooned, "So, Robert, now that you got us all buttered-up, what did you really bring us in for?" Everyone chuckled.

"Well," began Robert, "let me say, first of all, that I'm really pleased with all of the hard work that you folks have been putting into the changes we've been trying to institute. I've seen some real progress ... particularly in the way that you seem to be consistently using the greetings and expressions that we developed for our callers. The good news is that it looks like we're finally starting to see some 'pay-off' in terms of our clients' reaction to your efforts." Robert then told them about the latest Client Telephone Quality Report. He concluded by offering them his own personal "Congratulations!"

"Thank you for telling us that, Robert," Susan grinned.

"You're welcome, Susan," Robert replied. "But as you might suspect, we still have a lot of work to do in terms of 'delighting and amazing' our clients ... which is the other reason that I brought you in this morning. I need to find out something." Robert paused. "Tell me straight up ... right now, apart from the recent client survey, do either of you have any idea as to how well or poorly you are performing in terms of the goals on the mission task list?"

"I don't know what you mean," said Michael.

"Well, for instance, do you have any idea as to how well you are doing with respect to your goal of answering the phone within two rings?"

"I don't know," stammered Susan. "Maybe ninety percent."

"I would guess about the same." Michael responded.

Robert thought to himself, "Once again, the wise old man was right. They think that they're doing a pretty good job."

He then said to them, "Well, I'm sorry to have to tell you but I think that we have a bit of a problem here because that's not the impression that I've been getting. You see, I've been giving a lot of thought, these past few days, to the way that I've been monitoring you guys and the way that I've been giving you feedback. And I have come to the conclusion that it's been much too erratic and inconsistent ... that the method I've used really doesn't show me, or you, for that matter, whether you are improving or getting into difficulty ... and it doesn't allow me to see all the times when you've done something right."

"I'll agree with that," Michael interjected.

"So I've been doing some research and investigating a new technology that we can set up on our Agency's phone system to count the number of times our phones ring before they get answered as well as the number of seconds that a caller is put on hold. We can then generate for each of you a report at the end of every day indicating the number of times that you answered calls on the first ring, the second ring, the third ring, or four or more rings. The report will also tell you the average number of rings and the average number of seconds that a caller was kept on hold. That way, if we manage to answer the phones quickly but do so only at the cost of keeping our callers on hold too long, we'll know that we either need more staff or that we need to relax our two-ring policy."

"That's fantastic," Susan exclaimed. Michael's face grew solemn.

"The best part though," Robert continued, "is that with this system, it is ***totally objective and you can now keep track yourself of how well you are doing over time.*** We can also generate additional reports showing how quickly the phones are being answered on a daily, weekly and monthly basis. You can then ***use this information to monitor your own progress and see where any adjustments need to be made*** ... if there are any ... So, what do you think?"

"I love it," said Susan. "What do you think, Michael?"

"Well, if you want my honest opinion, Robert, it seems to me that we now have Big Brother watching us."

"I suppose that's one way of looking at it, Michael," replied Robert. "But there's another way as well. It's that we go back to my old method of monitoring performance which you just indicated that you didn't like either ... But, I'm totally open to suggestions. If you don't like the method that I'm proposing and can offer a better solution, then I am willing to hear about it and even to try it ... So tell me what you would propose instead?"

After a few moments of uncomfortable silence, Michael responded glumly, "Well, I guess we could try it your way to see how things go."

"That's the spirit Michael," Robert said enthusiastically. "But now comes the harder part. I still haven't been able to figure out a good system to monitor and count the number of times that you guys say a caller's name. I have some ideas but I'd sure love to hear how you both think that we should go about doing this. So, let's try to figure this one out together ...? Okay ...? ... Just like we did when we created the Mission Statement Task List."

"Okay, Robert." said Susan using her 'stage voice' again.

Robert then handed each team member a small pad of lined paper and asked them to write down all of their ideas to develop the new measurement system. After a very short while, the three of them had developed a system in which it was agreed that, Robert would:

- Listen in and record their phone calls for five minutes each day;

- Count the number of times that a client's name was mentioned during the calls;

- Evaluate their tone of voice quality on a scale of one to ten; and

- Prepare a weekly and monthly report showing the average, minimum and maximum number of times that each team member said a caller's name as well as the average voice tone quality rating.

- It was also agreed that Robert would let either team member listen to the tapes whenever they wanted to verify the 'caller name count' that he had recorded for them.

Robert then asked, "Do both of you think that this is a fair way of evaluating your performance while you execute the Agency's mission statement?"

"Completely." said Susan. "I really like these enhancements. Not only is it fair, it's also consistent and regular and it allows us to track our performance over time to see how we are doing." Michael, however, remained silent and only nodded his head.

"Well, then, let's see how it goes."

As it was time to open up the Agency's phone lines, Susan grabbed the remaining plate of food and both team members hurried towards their respective work stations.

Over the next several weeks, Robert followed through on the commitment that he had made with Michael and Susan in regards to measuring their performance and providing them with regular and consistent feedback.

As he had originally suspected, the first reports generated from the telephone system showed that neither Michael nor Susan were answering the phone anywhere near the levels that they had predicted. Susan, though, was proving to be the better performer. The reports showed that she was, on average, answering the phone within two (or less) rings about seventy five percent of the time. On the other hand, Michael's score was, according to Robert, an abysmal sixty-four percent.

But, just as the wise old man had predicted, the reports seemed to have their effect, at least insofar as Susan's performance was concerned. During the following three weeks, Susan's daily "two ring" percentage score increased to ninety-one percent and then appeared to "plateau". Michael's performance, on the other hand, stayed about the same - showing modest gains one week, only to be lost in the following measurement period.

The results concerning each person's performance in terms of saying a caller's name also proved to be not much different. When Susan first learned about her initial score (an average of three times per call), she became extremely motivated to, as she liked to put it, "beat her old record". Because of this, she managed to achieve a level of performance in which she was saying a caller's name an average of seven times. She also held the record for saying a caller's name the most number of times at fourteen. While Michael appeared to be trying to comply with this mission task, his efforts were, nonetheless, significantly below those of Susan.

The area that proved to be Michael's nemesis, though, was on the ratings he received for 'voice quality'. Susan remained true to her original voice training lessons and consistently applied the 'silky smooth' tones that she had learned to each and every call. It was becoming blatantly obvious, however, that Michael was just simply refusing to even try.

"It's just not me," he told Robert one afternoon as Robert was handing out the weekly performance results.

"I know it's not you, Michael," said Robert. "But, it's what you and Susan both agreed to do ... right? ... and it also seems to be something that the client appears to like and appreciate ... just ask Susan."

"I know that ... but, I still feel uncomfortable with what you keep asking me to do."

"I see," Robert replied. "But, surely you know by now **why** we need to be doing this ... right?"

"Yes, Robert," said Michael "to delight and amaze our clients in everything we do ... but I just don't like doing it, okay?"

"No Michael, it's not okay," replied Robert with a hint of impatience in his voice. "There are lots of things that we don't like to do in life but still have to do them anyway. So, think of this as one of those things."

Robert's voice then became almost pleading, "Look Michael, I really need you to try and get better at this. You need to know that our team needs you to do it ... Do you want me to arrange some refresher sessions with the voice coach for you?"

"No ... I know how to do it. I just have a problem getting my mind around doing it."

"Well, then," said Robert, "please know that I really need you to do it ... to embrace it. Susan's been able to. It looks bad on you if you don't as well. So, Michael, please try ... if not for yourself, then for me. I know you can do it if you really care."

But, things did not get much better.

It was then that Robert remembered the rest of the advice that the wise old man had given him - *to create personal* consequences for Michael and Susan for doing what they needed to do. To this end, he thought of several courses of action.

First, Robert announced that he was going to plot and publicly post their "combined" average score for the number of 'rings' on the wall in the hallway beside the Agency's production results. (The sales team's reports had been posted in that location for several years.) Posting their results would allow the Agency's other team members to see the degree to which Michael's and Susan's jobs were contributing to the Agency's mission and achieving the service standard that they had set for themselves. Because Susan would not want to have her score dragged down by Michael, Robert believed that with this approach, he could enlist Susan's support in helping to motivate Michael.

Robert also announced that at the end of each month he would declare in the company newsletter which of them scored the highest in terms of repeating a caller's name. Robert even bought a small trophy, which he hoped would rotate between the two team members, as a symbol of their friendly rivalry.

Finally, Robert thought that he should speak to Michael specifically about his voice quality problem once more. As he did so, Robert also informed

Michael that he would be revising his performance evaluation criteria to take Michael's voice quality score into account as part of his overall annual performance evaluation.

What happened next both surprised and depressed Robert.

Susan responded immediately to the challenges. So much so that she drove her performance score for answering the phone to record levels. She even managed to exceed the standard of two rings -which caused Robert to remark that "sooner or later Susan was going to start answering the phone before it even rang". But there was a down side to the success. Susan started to become antagonistic towards Michael - who she felt was not trying hard enough. "He's making the both of us look bad" Susan told Robert one day on his break. Indeed, posting their results also created mixed reactions amongst the Agency's other team members because Michael's and Susan's performance were so different.

Susan's performance in terms of saying a caller's name also defied all expectations. So much so, that it was becoming obvious after the second month that only Susan would ever be the possessor of the trophy. Michael's view, however, was now becoming characteristic. He said that he simply didn't care about such "baubles" - as he put it.

While Robert was delighted with the progress

that he had made in helping Susan finally do what the Agency and its mission statement needed her to do, he was also at odds with Michael's response to all of his efforts. "I've done everything that the wise old man told me to do," he thought to himself. "Yet, I've only managed to succeed with Susan and not with Michael." He could not explain the differences in outcomes that he had achieved. Robert, therefore, promised himself that he would take the next available opportunity to see Philip and to find out what additional wisdom the wise old man might have for him this time ...

Philip's Final Lesson

As Robert explained the situation to the wise old man, Philip listened patiently. When Robert was finished the wise old man repeated his usual litany of questions to him. Only this time the focus was exclusively on Michael.

"Does he *know what to do?*" came Philip's traditional opening remark.

"Of course he does," shot back Robert. "Michael can recite the mission and mission task list flawlessly."

"And does he *know why he should do what you want him to do?*" came the second round.

"Without question. I've asked him to tell me '*the why*' dozens of times. He knows '*the why*'," said Robert with a hint of anger growing in his voice.

"And, does he *know how to do it?*" fired back Philip.

"Yes, he most certainly does," answered Robert. "Now, look here Philip ..."

Philip, however, seemed to not even notice Robert's festering annoyance. "And does he *know that he should care* about doing what you need him to do?"

"Definitely!" replied Robert, almost shouting now. "Philip, listen to everything that I've just told you. I've recounted for you all the things that I've done to try and make Michael feel that he should care and still, I'm not getting the behavior or the results that I need from Michael. What have I done wrong?" Robert's anger was turning into exasperation.

"Well, my clever young man," came Philip's terse response, "The answer to your question is simple. It's that you haven't done anything wrong. The problem now no longer lies with you to solve ... the problem lies with Michael himself ... and, it appears that *he just doesn't get it!*"

"What do you mean 'he just doesn't get it'?" asked Robert somewhat confused at Philip's cryptic words.

"I mean that Michael's personal internal value system and attitudes appear to be so damaged or corrupted that despite your best efforts to show him *'the what'*, *'the why'*, *'the how'* and *'to care'*, he is prepared to dig in his heels and defy your best attempts to help assist him ... His poor values and attitudes also appear to be so entrenched that it might take you many more months - and maybe even years - to try and reverse them ... and unfortunately for Michael, you probably don't have that amount of time to devote to him ... or do you?

"Not really, Philip," replied Robert.

"Well then, you should probably have a pretty good idea as to what it is that you have to do with him. You see, Robert, the world is full of people like Michael. Your challenge as a leader, therefore, is to avoid - or get rid of - all of 'the Michaels' that you encounter and to find, keep and motivate as many of 'the Susans' as you can."

Robert looked dejected.

"What's wrong, Robert?"

"It's just that I feel badly about Michael. That somehow I failed him."

"Robert, you didn't fail Michael. He failed himself." Philip took a deep breath and continued, "Robert, you're a talented young leader ... and I admire you greatly. But, despite your inexperience, you can't ever allow yourself to forget the most important leadership principle."

"The most important leadership principle? ...What's that?" asked Robert.

"It's that when team members are not doing what it is that needs to be done ... not doing what they were *hired* to do, **great leaders always blame themselves first**. They say to themselves: 'this problem is my problem ... now what can I do about it?

"When it comes to difficult team members, leaders ask themselves, '*Do they know what to do?*', '*Do they know why they should be doing it?*' '*Do they know how to do it?*' and '*Do they know that they should care?*' ... and if they can answer "yes" to all four of those questions, then great leaders accept the fact that somehow 'a Michael' made it into their ranks, someone who ... **just doesn't get it**, and only then do they not blame themselves first ... unless of course they hired 'the Michael' in the first place...which then might mean they have a problem with the way they recruit people. So, go deal with 'your Michael' and start looking for another 'Susan'. Do you see what I'm saying?"

"I think so." replied Robert.

"Good ... then go forth and prosper, Robert ... and now get the heck out of here because I have a lot of work to do."

Robert rose from the chair in which he was sitting and thanked Philip profusely for all of his patience and coaching. Robert sensed, somewhat wistfully, though, that his days of running to see the wise old man were at an end ... that Philip had succeeded in teaching him the most important leadership principle ... and that now all he had to do was practice it ... over and over and over.

He promised himself that he would not disappoint

his old mentor and that he would master the ways of leadership as Philip had helped him to learn.

When Robert returned to his office he summarized what Philip had taught him as follows:

The 'Don't Know' Theory of Leadership

There are **only five reasons** why team members might not do what you need them to do...

It's because they ...

i) Don't know **WHAT** to do.

ii) Don't know **WHY** they should do it.

iii) Don't know **HOW** to do it.

iv) Don't know that they should **CARE**.

v) Don't **GET IT**.

A good leader makes sure that a team member knows the first four things before he concludes that the team member 'doesn't get it'.

A great leader always ***blames himself first***.

Epilogue

The next day Robert asked Michael to see him after work. The two men had an open and honest conversation about what Robert needed Michael to do and what Michael was prepared to give. In light of everything that he had learned the past several months from Philip, it came as no surprise when Michael stated that he was very unhappy with his current job and that he wanted a change. Robert promised to help Michael find another position that was more to his liking and attitude. Michael thanked Robert with a sincerity that the clever young man had never seen before.

Both men went home that evening feeling good about themselves.

****

Two years passed. Philip retired. Susan married one of the Agency's clients. And Robert's Agency grew by leaps and bounds. By now, Robert had earned quite a reputation for himself within the company and among fellow Agents. He was known as someone who knew how to get the job done....who knew how to make his agency's mission matter and to make it come alive. His Agency had even managed to win the company's overall 'client satisfaction award'. Everyone called him a natural born leader.

Then, one day, as he was beginning to settle into

his new expanded office, a knock came at the door. It was Patricia Reeves. She had just graduated from Agency School and had been given the opportunity to run a small rural agency. It was her first time leading a team and Robert thought of her as a clever young woman.

She asked, "Can you spare me a few moments, Robert?"

"Sure," came Robert's reply. "What can I do for you?"

"Well," she began, "I've got this new Agency assignment with some relatively new team members who are not doing what I need them to do and I was wondering if you could give me some advice on how I might help them to become more engaged?"

"I see," said the now wise, but still quite young, Robert. "I'll certainly try. So, tell me, Patricia, *do they know what to do?* ..."

THE END

Dr. Chris Bart, FCPA

Dr. Chris Bart, FCPA is the world's leading expert on organizational mission statements (the most widely used management tool in the world) and how companies can use them more effectively to become a "mission driven" organization. He is currently the CEO of Corporate Missions Inc – an international consulting firm dedicated to helping organizations excel in the execution of their strategies. He is the also the Founder of The Directors College where from its inception in 2003 to 2013, he served as its inaugural Principal and Lead Professor. He now assists the College as its Lead Faculty and pursues his passion for good governance globally as the Co- Founder and Executive Chairman of the Caribbean Governance Training Institute in Saint Lucia.

Dr. Bart has authored the 10 year Canadian business best seller (2003-2013), "A Tale of Two Team members and the Person Who Wanted to Lead Them" as well as the widely acclaimed publications: "20 Essential Questions Corporate Directors Should

Ask About Strategy (2013) – 3rd Edition" and "20 Essential Questions Directors of Not-For-Profit Organizations Should Ask About Strategy (2009). Organizations Should Ask About Strategy (2009). He also has recently released two new books: "Achieving the Execution Edge: 20 Essential Questions Corporate Directors Need to Get Answered About Strategy Execution" (with E.S. Schreiber); and "The Mission Driven Hospital: Turning Noble Aspirations through Accountability and Action".

Through his pioneering research and teachings, Dr. Bart has become highly sought after by organizations seeking to develop vision and mission statements that get results. His practical approach for bringing mission state- ments to life has inspired business leaders and audiences around the world.

A retired Professor of Strategy and Governance from McMaster University (1981-2013), Dr. Bart has published over 170 articles, cases and reviews. He currently serves as Associate Editor of the International Journal of Business Governance & Ethics and he continues as a Research Fellow of the Asian Institute of Corporate Governance at Korea University. Previously, he helped establish the Management of Innovation and New Technology Research Centre (MINT~RC) at McMaster and was named its first Director.

Dr. Bart has been awarded the Ontario Chamber

of Commerce "Outstanding Business Achievement Award for Corporate Governance", the Hamilton Chamber of Commerce "HR Hero Award", the United Way "Chairman's Award", the HRPA 2011 "Summit Award for Corporate Governance & Strategic Leadership", and McMaster's "Innovation Award". For his research, he has received both the McMaster Research Recognition Award and its Theory to Practice Award. A highly regarded lecturer, Dr. Bart has received both the "Outstanding Undergraduate Business Professor" and "MBA Professor of the Year" awards on multiple occasions. He has also won "The President's Award for Teaching Excellence", McMaster's highest teaching award – which made him the most decorated professor at the DeGroote School. In 2009, his CPA designation was elevated to FCPA (Fellow of the Institute of Chartered Professional Accountants). And in 2012, Dr. Bart was the recipient of the Queen Elizabeth II Diamond Jubilee Medal for his service to Canada.

Over the years, Dr. Bart has been invited to lecture at numerous institutions throughout the world, including the USA, South Africa, Egypt, Greece, the Caribbean, Switzerland, the United Kingdom, Australia, the Czech Republic and China.

Dr. Bart is listed in Canadian Who's Who. He is currently a Trustee of the Committee for Economic Development of the United States of America and a Director of Terra Firma Capital Corporation (TII.V) where he serves on the firm's Audit Committee and chairs the Governance, Compensation and Nominating Committee. He is a past Director of St. Joseph's Hospital, the Harshman Foundation, The Canadian Foundation for Education and Research on Finance, the United Way of Burlington and Greater Hamilton and Eagle Precision Technologies (a former TSE listed company) where he chaired its Compensation Committee.

To contact Dr Bart:

Phone: 905 – 515 - 6399
e-mail: chrisbart@corporatemissionsinc.com
            www.corporatemissionsinc.com

Wayne Nichols

Wayne Nichols is an independent Insurance and Financial Services Agent who has been serving the Golden Horseshoe from the town of Dundas, Ontario since 1994. Representing State Farm Insurance Companies for more than twenty years and Desjardins Insurance Companies since 2015, Wayne has provided outstanding expertise to his clients.

Early in his Insurance career Wayne was a Commissioner for Taking Affidavits. Wayne acquired four years of Insurance claims experience prior to opening his Insurance and Financial Services business. Wayne is a member of the Insurance Institute of Canada and a past member of Advocis - The Financial Advisors Association of Canada.

Wayne has consistently been recognized as one of the leading agents for State Farm Insurance Companies. He has qualified for the State Farm President's Club twenty-four times in his career, an accomplishment that only a few agents will ever achieve. Wayne is also honored to be a Lifetime

Member of the President's Club, a qualification that a select few State Farm agents achieve. Wayne has been recognized for many years as achieving a ranking in the top 50 State Farm agents out of the more than 18,000 State Farm agents throughout Canada and the United States. At one point in his career Wayne was ranked as the #1 Mutual Fund representative for State Farm Insurance companies.

Today Wayne and his team represent Desjardin Insurance products under the State Farm brand. They continue to lead in a Canadian sales team for Desjardins Insurance.

Over the years, Wayne has devoted many hours to the ongoing success of not only his business, but also to that of State Farm and many of his fellow agents. He and his knowledgeable team continue to service clients throughout the province of Ontario with fast, friendly and professional advice for all insurance and financial services needs.

Since graduating together from The University of Western Ontario, Wayne and his wife Stephanie have supported each other. Stephanie has always assisted in the growth and development of their Insurance Agency. Their two daughters, Christine and Heather are continuously motivated by the commitment and passion their father displays.

To Contact Wayne:

Phone: 905 628-36565 ext 4
Email: wayne@waynenichols.ca
             www.waynenichols.ca

www.ingramcontent.com/pod-product-compliance
Lightning Source LLC
Chambersburg PA
CBHW042121190326
41519CB00031B/7575